8TH GRADE
ENGLISH AND LANGUAGE ARTS
Unit 10
Drama: *The Miracle Worker*

Table of Contents

Leadership 101
Initiative

*Recognizing and doing what needs to be done
before I am asked to do it*

ResponsiveEd® thanks Character First (www.characterfirst.com) for permission to integrate its character resources into this Unit.

- Read with fluency and comprehension.

- Understand, make inferences, and draw conclusions about the structure and elements of drama and provide evidence from the text to support understanding.

- Use a dictionary or thesaurus to determine the meanings of words.

- Analyze, make inferences, and draw conclusions about the theme and genre of a literary work.

- Understand, make inferences, and draw conclusions about the structure and elements of fiction and provide evidence from text to support understanding.

- Analyze how playwrights characterize their protagonists and antagonists through the dialogue and staging of their plays.

- Gather information from a range of relevant print and electronic sources.

- Analyze how the central characters' qualities influence the theme of a fictional work and resolution of the central conflict.

- Analyze linear plot developments to determine whether and how conflicts are resolved.

- Analyze different forms of point of view.

- Understand, make inferences, and draw conclusions about how an author's sensory language creates imagery in a literary text.

- Use context to determine or clarify the meanings of unfamiliar words.

- Explain how the values and beliefs of particular characters are affected by the historical and cultural setting of the literary work.

- Write responses to literary texts that demonstrate the use of writing skills for a multi-paragraph essay and provide sustained evidence from the text using quotations when appropriate.

WHAT IS INITIATIVE?

Have you ever carried a heavy load of books or tried to open a door with your arms full, and no one noticed or offered to help? When people lack initiative, they fail to see needs that should be obvious.

Initiative helps others, but it will also help you. It can get you ahead in school, improve life at home, and secure a better future.

1. INTRODUCTION TO DRAMA; ACT I, SCENES i–ii

Objectives:

- Read with fluency and comprehension.
- Understand, make inferences, and draw conclusions about the structure and elements of drama and provide evidence from the text to support understanding.
- Use a dictionary or thesaurus to determine the meanings of words.
- Analyze, make inferences, and draw conclusions about the theme and genre of a literary work.
- Understand, make inferences, and draw conclusions about the structure and elements of fiction and provide evidence from text to support understanding.
- Gather information from a range of relevant print and electronic sources.

Vocabulary:

act – a major unit in a drama

aside – a comment or statement that a character makes directly to the audience or another character but is not "heard" by other characters onstage

cast – a list of characters in a play

comedy – a type of drama that is humorous and usually has a happy ending

dialogue – words spoken by characters onstage

drama – a genre of literature that is written to be performed by actors on a stage in front of an audience

dramatic irony – occurs when the audience knows something that the characters onstage do not

playwright – a person who writes the text of a play

scene – a division of an act that has a specific time and place

script – the written text of a play

stage directions – instructions for performing the drama, including descriptions of characters' actions

tragedy – a serious drama in which a major character suffers a downfall or catastrophe because of wrong decisions or foolish actions

INTRODUCTION TO DRAMA

So far this year, you have studied many different genres of literature, including fiction short stories and novels, literary nonfiction, informational texts, speeches, and poetry. The final genre you will study this year is **drama**. You may already have an idea in your mind about what drama is. The word *drama* may be in your everyday vocabulary ("She's such a drama queen!"). However, the type of drama we will discuss in this Unit is the genre of literature that is written to be performed by actors on a stage in front of an audience. A person who writes a drama or play is called a **playwright**.

What makes drama different from other genres of literature? To begin with, drama uses **dialogue** (words spoken by characters onstage) and **stage directions** (instructions for performing the drama, including descriptions of characters' actions) to tell the story. Stage directions can include movements, actions, sounds, special effects, lighting, or other elements that add to the dialogue. Stage directions are usually written in italics and enclosed by parentheses. Rather than using description to give a mental picture to the reader, a drama allows an audience to actually see the actions, personalities, and physical characteristics of characters played by actors and actresses. The **script** is the written text of a play, including dialogue and stage directions, as well as a list of characters, or **cast**. In reading a script of a play, the stage directions are just as important as the dialogue. Do not skip over the stage directions.

Plays are divided into major units called **acts**. These acts are often divided into smaller segments called **scenes**. Each scene has its own specific setting. Scene divisions are usually based on changes in time, place, or situation.

Dramas can be categorized into sub-genres. A **comedy** is a type of drama that is humorous and usually has a happy ending, while a **tragedy** is a serious drama in which a major character suffers a downfall or catastrophe because of wrong decisions or foolish actions. Dramas can be based on fiction or nonfiction stories. A historical drama is based on a significant, real-life event or person in history. While most historical dramas seek to accurately and truthfully portray events and people, some historical dramas contain nonfactual elements. Though the event portrayed in a historical drama may be one that actually happened, some of the dialogue and situations are most likely creatively added to make the drama more appealing.

A common element of traditional drama is an **aside**—a comment or statement that a character makes directly to the audience or another character but is not "heard" by other characters onstage. Often, an aside is intended to reveal a character's inner thoughts and feelings. While used frequently in older dramas, asides are not very common in modern plays.

In previous Units you have studied irony, a contrast between expectation and reality, and you have read stories that use irony. Dramas often contain **dramatic irony**, which occurs when the audience knows something that the characters onstage do not. Often, playwrights and directors stage plays so that the audience has a clear view of all the action that takes place, but the characters themselves may not be fully aware of all the events that occur onstage. For example, in one scene, the audience witnesses a character committing a crime. In another scene, a detective unknowingly asks the villain if he knows who committed the crime, and the villain gives the detective false information. The audience knows something that the detective does not. Another example of dramatic irony occurs in the short story, "The Ransom of Red Chief." Red Chief, the little boy who was kidnapped, becomes a terror to his kidnappers. When the kidnappers try to get rid of Red Chief, and they think they are successful in doing so, the narrator informs the reader that the boy is actually standing right behind one of the kidnappers. The narrator gives information to the reader that at least one of the characters in the story does not know. In another story you have read this year, "The Cask of Amontillado," the reader knows that Montresor is seeking revenge by planning to murder Fortunato, but Fortunato is not aware that he is in danger.

As you read the drama in this Unit, you will need to understand the drama terms discussed in this Lesson. In addition to the elements of drama, plays contain elements of fiction stories, such as plot, conflict, setting, characters, and theme.

INTRODUCTION TO *THE MIRACLE WORKER*

The play you will be reading throughout this Unit is *The Miracle Worker* by William Gibson. It recounts the true story of Helen Keller and the influence of her teacher, Anne Sullivan. You are probably familiar with some details about the life of Helen Keller; however, it is necessary to build background information before beginning to read the play. You will perform research to gain background knowledge of Helen Keller and Anne Sullivan.

Helen Keller and Anne Sullivan

ACTIVITY: BACKGROUND RESEARCH

Using a print or electronic source, such as a book, an encyclopedia, or a website, locate the answers to the questions.

1.1) When and where was Helen Keller born?

When: _____

Where: _____

1.2) How did Helen become deaf and blind? _____

_____

1.3) How old was Helen when she became deaf and blind? _____

1.4) How old was Helen when Anne Sullivan began tutoring her? _____

1.5) What college did Helen attend? _____ _____

1.6) Why is her graduation from college significant? _____

_____

1.7) What book did Helen Keller write when she was 22 years old? _____

_____

1.8) Describe Helen and Anne's relationship after Helen graduated from college. _____

_____

_____

1.9) How old was Helen when she died? _____

1.10) What tragedy did Anne Sullivan experience at the age of 5? _____

_____

1.11) Describe what happened to Anne's mother and father. _____

_____

_____

1.12) Where did Anne live when she was young? _____

1.13) How old was Anne when she became Helen's teacher? _____

1.14) Discuss Anne's married life. _____

_____

Check Correct Recheck

CONNECTING TO THE TEXT

Now that you know a little information about Helen Keller, try to put yourself in her shoes. You have probably never experienced deafness or blindness, so it may be difficult for you to relate to these individuals as you read about them in the play. Consider how your world would be different if you were deprived of both of your senses of sight and hearing.

Write a paragraph connecting to the text.

1.15) In a well-developed paragraph, describe how you think your world would be different if you were unable to see or hear. Describe the things you would miss the most. Discuss how you would communicate with your friends, your family, and others. How do you think you would feel going out in public knowing you had an obvious disability? How would you express your feelings and ideas? Discuss these issues and questions and include any other observations you have concerning this topic.

_____

_____

_____

_____

_____

_____

_____

Teacher Check

PRE-READING VOCABULARY

Before you begin reading *The Miracle Worker*, look up the words in a dictionary and write a correct definition for each word. Many of the following words describe the manner in which a character speaks. For example, in the first scene, the doctor speaks *amiably* to Captain and Mrs. Keller. Since you are reading the play instead of watching it, you need to understand what tone the characters use as they speak. As you read, be aware of how these words are used in the text.

1.16) amiably – _____

1.17) indulgent – _____

1.18) jovial – _____

1.19) benign – _____

1.20) oculist – _____

1.21) facetiously – _____

1.22) asylum – _____

1.23) placating – _____

1.24) inexorably – _____

Check   Correct   Recheck

5

MENTALLY STAGING THE PLAY

Most often, this play is performed on a traditional stage with a proscenium *[proh-SEE-nee-uhm]* arch, which looks like a big picture frame that surrounds the play and separates the stage from the audience. In a proscenium stage, the audience directly faces the stage. Other types of theaters have the audience surrounding the stage or on three sides of the stage.

Proscenium arch

As you read the play, it is necessary for you to have a mental picture of the setting as if you were watching the play being performed. The drama script should include a description of the stage, or playing space. Read the description, and you will notice that the stage is divided into two parts by an imaginary diagonal line that extends from the left corner of the close side of the stage (from the audience's perspective) to the right corner of the far side of the stage. The Keller house is always behind the diagonal line throughout the play. The area in front of the diagonal line serves as every other setting in the play, such as the Keller's yard, the Perkins Institute for the Blind, and the train station. Try to keep a mental image of the action and imagine what it would look like if you were watching a staged version of the play.

Now, look at the list of characters that will participate in the drama. The characters are listed in the order that they appear in the play. On the same page, the setting is described for you. As you can see, the play takes place in the 1880s, and the action occurs at the Keller home in Tuscumbia, Alabama, as well as the Perkins Institute for the Blind in Boston, Massachusetts.

You will now begin reading the play. *The Miracle Worker* is divided into three acts. Each act contains several scene changes, but the scenes are not marked. Each scene change involves a change in time or place. For each Lesson, you will be reading two or three scenes. Pay close attention to where the scenes begin and end to ensure that you are reading the correct material for each Lesson.

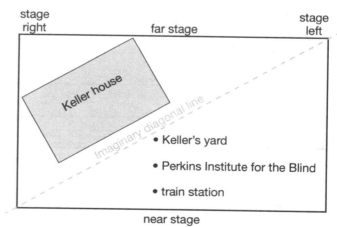

Stage setting for *The Miracle Worker*

📖 **Read Act I, Scenes i-ii of *The Miracle Worker*.**

- Scene i – Helen as a toddler
  - ☞ Begin your reading with, *"It is night over the Keller homestead."*

- Scene ii – Helen as a six-year-old
  - ☞ End your reading with, *"The lights dim out, except the one on KATE and*

HELEN. *In the twilight,* JAMES, AUNT EV *and* KELLER *move off slowly, formally in separate directions;* KATE *with* HELEN *in her arms remains, motionless, in an image which overlaps into the next scene and fades only when it is well under way."*

Review

Write the correct answers from Act I, Scenes i–ii.

1.25) Describe the three characters standing over the crib at the beginning of Scene i.

    a. Kate – _____

    b. doctor – _____

    c. Captain Keller – _____

1.26) What kind of mood is present at the beginning of Scene i, and how does the mood change?

_____

_____

1.27) When does Kate Keller first realize that something is wrong? _____

_____

_____

1.28) Describe how Helen behaves toward Percy and Martha in Scene ii. _____

_____

_____

1.29) What bothers Helen about the doll Aunt Ev gives her in Scene ii? _____

_____

1.30) What can you infer about the relationship between James and Captain Keller, his father? How does James feel about Helen? Refer to specific lines or stage directions from the play in your answer. _____

_____

_____

_____

1.31) What does Helen do that causes her father to say that she must be confined? _____

_____

1.32) What does Captain Keller decide to do? _____

_____

Write the correct drama term next to the statement which describes it using words from the box below.

comedy	scene	historical drama	tragedy	act
dialogue	aside	stage directions	script	
playwright	cast	dramatic irony	drama	

1.33) _____ – a major unit in a drama

1.34) _____ – a person who writes the text of a play

1.35) _____ – a comment or statement that a character makes directly to the audience or another character but is not "heard" by other characters onstage

1.36) _____ – a genre of literature that is written to be performed by actors on a stage in front of an audience

1.37) _____ – occurs when the audience knows something that the characters onstage do not

1.38) _____ – a list of characters in a play

1.39) _____ – instructions for performing the drama, including descriptions of characters' actions

1.40) _____ – a type of drama that is humorous and usually has a happy ending

1.41) _____ – a division of an act that has a specific time and place

1.42) _____ – a serious drama in which a major character suffers a downfall or catastrophe because of wrong decisions or foolish actions

1.43) _____ – the written text of a play

1.44) _____ – words spoken by characters onstage

1.45) _____ – based on a significant, real-life event or person in history; may contain nonfactual or creative elements

Check   Correct   Recheck

2. ACT I, SCENES iii–iv

Objectives:

- Read with fluency and comprehension.
- Understand, make inferences, and draw conclusions about the structure and elements of drama and provide evidence from the text to support understanding.
- Use a dictionary or thesaurus to determine the meanings of words.
- Gather information from a range of relevant print and electronic sources.
- Analyze how playwrights characterize their protagonists and antagonists through the dialogue and staging of their plays.
- Analyze how the central characters' qualities influence the theme of a fictional work and resolution of the central conflict.

Vocabulary:

antagonist *[an-TAG-uh-nist]* – a character who opposes the protagonist

flashback – interruptions in the action to present events that took place in the past

protagonist *[proh-TAG-uh-nist]* – central character of the drama

In reading the first two scenes of Act I, you got a quick glimpse into the lives of the Keller family. It is clear that something must be done to help Helen. She is undisciplined and unruly, and she causes danger to those around her, like Martha and her sister Mildred. Consider, for a moment, the motivation behind Helen's actions. Do you think she acts the way she does to purposely cause harm to others? Does she realize how her actions are perceived?

Try to put yourself in Helen's situation. How would you express your feelings if you could not communicate verbally or visually? How would you react if you could not understand anything anyone said, and you had no way to communicate your thoughts and feelings? As a six-year-old who has been blind and deaf since before she was two years old, Helen does not understand the world around her, and so far, she has had no one to teach her. She lives in darkness, silence, and confusion.

The following excerpt is from Helen Keller's autobiography, *The Story of My Life*. In this passage, Helen describes her frustrations with communication before Anne Sullivan came to her.

I do not remember when I first realized that I was different from other people; but I knew it before my teacher came to me. I had noticed that my mother and my friends did not use signs as I did when they wanted anything done, but talked with their mouths. Sometimes I stood between two persons who were conversing and touched their lips. I could not understand, and was **vexed [irritated]**. I moved my lips and **gesticulated [gestured]** frantically without result. This made me so angry at times that I kicked and screamed until I was exhausted.

I think I knew when I was naughty, for I knew that it hurt Ella, my nurse, to kick her, and when my fit of temper was over I had a feeling akin to regret. But I cannot remember any instance in which this feeling prevented me from repeating the naughtiness when I failed to get what I wanted.

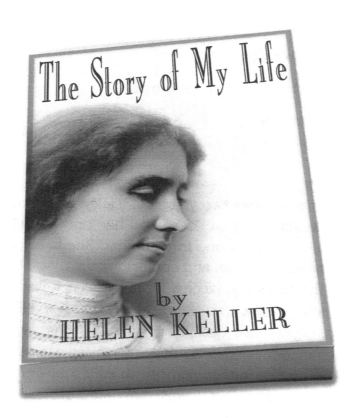

CHARACTERIZATION AND INFERENCES

In the reading for this Lesson, you will be introduced to the main character of the play, Annie Sullivan. She is the **protagonist**, or central character, of the drama. Throughout the play, she encounters several **antagonists**, or characters who oppose her. The manner in which she responds to these antagonistic forces will reveal a great deal about her character.

In order to chart the development of different characters throughout the drama, you must make inferences based on their words, actions and responses. So far in the play, you have sensed the tension between James and his father, Captain Keller, as well as James' disdain for his half-sister, Helen. From what you have read, you can also infer that Captain Keller does not know how to behave toward Helen, and he does not believe anyone can help her. His wife, Kate, holds out hope that Helen can be taught, and she seems to be the most sympathetic of all Helen's family members.

In the next two scenes of Act I, you will continue to make inferences about the characters based on their words and actions. Look for **flashbacks** (interruptions in the action to present events that took place in the past) the main character experiences, and try to determine what these flashbacks reveal about her. Pay attention to how characters are described, as well as their words and actions.

PRE-READING VOCABULARY
Look up the words in a dictionary and write a definition for each.

2.1) obstinate – _____

2.2) precocious – _____

2.3) tantrum – _____

2.4) crescendo – _____

2.5) desiccated – _____

2.6) spinster – _____

2.7) sotto voce – _____

Check   Correct   Recheck

📖 **Read Act I, Scene iii of *The Miracle Worker*.**

Scene iii – at the Perkins School for the Blind, in Boston

☞ Begin your reading with, *"Without pause, from the dark down left we hear a man's voice with a Greek accent speaking."*

☞ End your reading with, *"This word catches* KATE, *who stands half turned and attentive to it, almost as though hearing it. Meanwhile,* ANNIE *turns and hurries out, lugging the suitcase."*

Review

Write the correct answers from Act I, Scene iii.

2.8) How does the playwright characterize Annie in the first description of her? _____

_____

_____

2.9) What does Anagnos imply about Annie's past? _____

_____

_____

2.10) How does Annie respond when Anagnos tells her that Helen throws tantrums often?

_____

_____

2.11) What did the Perkins School for the Blind do for Annie? _____

_____

_____

2.12) What present do the blind children give to Annie as a going-away gift? _____

_____

2.13) Describe the flashback Annie experiences in Act I, Scene iii. _____

_____

_____

_____

_____

Read Act I, Scene iv of *The Miracle Worker*.

Scene iv – at the Keller home and on the way home from the train station

☞ Begin where you left off at the end of Scene iii.

☞ End your reading with, *"She goes into the house, and through the rear door of the family room.* JAMES *trudges in with the trunk, takes it up the steps to* ANNIE'S *room, and sets it down outside the door. The lights elsewhere dim somewhat."*

As you read Act I, Scene iv of *The Miracle Worker*, you will make inferences about the characters in the scene, specifically Annie, Kate, James, and Captain Keller. Consider specifically the actions of the protagonist and the other characters' reactions toward her.

For each of the characters listed in **Table 2.1**, you will make inferences based on the dialogue and stage directions of the scene. Examples of dialogue/stage directions are listed for you. Read the dialogue and/or stage directions. They reveal something about the characters listed. Then, write the inferences you make from the dialogue/stage directions in the third column of the table.

Review

Complete the chart by making inferences about characters based on their dialogue.

TABLE 2.1		
Character	**Dialogue/Stage Directions**	**Inference** **(what the dialogue/stage directions** **tell me about that character)**
Kate	**KATE**: Here. For while I'm gone. *(HELEN sniffs, reaches, and pops something into her mouth, while KATE speaks a bit guiltily.)* I don't think one peppermint drop will spoil your supper.	**Example**: Kate knows that Helen will probably throw a temper tantrum, so she gives her a piece of candy to pacify Helen while Kate is gone. She bribes Helen with candy because she does not know how to discipline her.
	(Now she [Kate] voices part of her doubt, not as such, but ANNIE understands it.) **KATE**: I expected—a desiccated spinster. You're very young. **KATE**: May I ask how old you are?	2.14)
	KATE: I like her, Captain. **KELLER**: Certainly rear a peculiar kind of young woman in the north. How old is she? **KATE** [VAGUELY]: Ohh—Well, she's not in her teens, you know.	2.15)

Annie		
ANNIE: You—live far from town, Mrs. Keller? **KATE**: Only a mile. **ANNIE**: Well. I suppose I can wait one more mile. But don't be surprised if I get out to push the horse!	2.16)	
KATE: We can't get through to teach her to sit still. You are young, despite your years, to have such—confidence. Do you, inside? (*ANNIE studies her face; she likes her, too.*) **ANNIE**: No, to tell you the truth I'm as shaky inside as a baby's rattle!	2.17)	
KATE: We'll do all we can to help, and to make you feel at home. Don't think of us as strangers, Miss Annie. **ANNIE** [CHEERILY]: Oh, strangers aren't so strange to me. I've known them all my life!	2.18)	

James		
JAMES: I'm moving your—Mrs. Keller, instead. To the station. **KELLER**: Mrs. Keller. Must you always speak of her as though you haven't met the lady? *(KATE comes out on the porch, and JAMES inclines his head.)* **JAMES** [IRONIC]: Mother. *(He starts off the porch, but sidesteps KELLER'S glare like a blow.)*	2.19)	
ANNIE: James? *(The name stops her.)* I had a brother Jimmie. Are you Helen's? **JAMES**: I'm only half a brother. You're to be her governess? **ANNIE** [LIGHTLY]: Well. Try! **JAMES** [EYEING HER]: You look like half a governess.	2.20)	

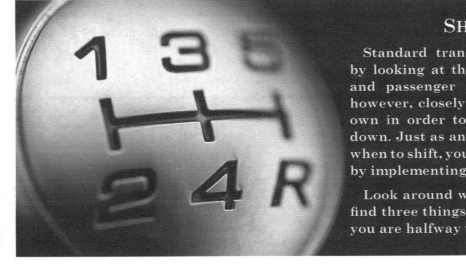

SHIFTING GEARS

Standard transmissions are easily recognized by looking at the shift lever between the driver and passenger seats. Automatic transmissions, however, closely monitor vehicle factors on their own in order to determine when to shift up or down. Just as an automatic transmission initiates when to shift, you can make life run more smoothly by implementing the character trait of initiative.

Look around wherever you are sitting. Can you find three things that need to be done? If you can, you are halfway to learning initiative!

Captain Keller	KELLER: She's [Kate's] gone. *(He is awkward with her; when he puts his hand on her head, she pulls away. KELLER stands regarding her, heavily.)* She's gone, my son and I don't get along, you don't know I'm your father, no one likes me, and supper's delayed.	2.21)
	KELLER: *And* the suitcase— ANNIE [PLEASANTLY]: I'll take the suitcase thanks. KELLER: Not at all, I have it, Miss Sullivan. ANNIE: I'd like it. KELLER [GALLANTLY]: I couldn't think of it, Miss Sullivan. You'll find in the south we— ANNIE: Let me. KELLER: —view women as the flowers of civiliza— ANNIE [IMPATIENTLY]: I've got something in it for Helen! *(She tugs it free; KELLER stares.)*	2.22)
	KELLER: Here's a houseful of grownups can't cope with the child, how can an inexperienced half-blind Yankee schoolgirl manage her?	2.23)

Check   Correct   Recheck

ACTIVITY: PERFORMING BACKGROUND RESEARCH

In this section of the play, Annie comments that she has studied the works of Dr. Howe, a well-known educator of the blind. He is famous for being the first person to successfully educate a deaf-blind person, a girl named Laura Bridgman, decades before Helen Keller was born. Search for information about these two individuals, Dr. Samuel Howe and Laura Bridgman, to answer the following questions. The website for the Perkins School for the Blind presents information that would help you answer these questions. You may need to consult more than one source.

Laura Bridgman

Dr. Samuel Howe

Answer the questions.

2.24) What was Dr. Howe's role at the Perkins Institute? _____

_____

2.25) What did Laura Bridgman and Helen Keller have in common? _____

_____

_____

2.26) What famous author wrote of Dr. Howe's work with Laura Bridgman?

_____   _____

2.27) How was Laura Bridgman's legacy influential in Helen Keller's education? _____

_____

_____

2.28) What connection does Mr. Anagnos, Annie's former teacher, have with Dr. Howe? _____

_____

_____

Check   Correct   Recheck

3. ACT I, SCENES v–vi

Objectives:

- Read with fluency and comprehension.
- Understand, make inferences, and draw conclusions about the structure and elements of drama and provide evidence from the text to support understanding.
- Use a dictionary or thesaurus to determine the meanings of words.
- Analyze how playwrights characterize their protagonists and antagonists through the dialogue and staging of their plays.
- Analyze how the central characters' qualities influence the theme of a fictional work and resolution of the central conflict.
- Analyze linear plot developments to determine whether and how conflicts are resolved.
- Analyze different forms of point of view.
- Understand, make inferences, and draw conclusions about how an author's sensory language creates imagery in a literary text.

Vocabulary:

idiom *[ID-ee-uhm]* – a figurative phrase whose meaning is not related to the literal meaning of its words; an expression common to a particular group of people

PROTAGONISTS AND ANTAGONISTS

In Lesson 2, you learned that Anne Sullivan is the protagonist of this story. As she arrives to the Keller home, she is somewhat nervous, but overall, she displays cheerfulness, optimism, and confidence. However, the other characters, especially Captain Keller, are not quite so confident in her abilities. In the last section of Act I, you will begin to see which characters act antagonistic toward Anne.

IDIOMS IN *THE MIRACLE WORKER*

Throughout the play, characters often use **idioms**—phrases whose meanings are not related to the literal meanings of the words. Idioms are often characteristic of a particular group of people; for example, a person from the South may use different idioms than a person who lives in the North. An example of an idiom is spoken by Captain Keller in Act I. He makes the statement, "The house is at *sixes* and *sevens* from morning till night over the child . . ." The phrase, at *sixes* and *sevens*, is an idiom that means "in a state of confusion and disorder." As you can see, the words that make up the phrase have nothing to do with the meaning of the phrase itself.

PRE-READING VOCABULARY

Look up the words in a dictionary and write a definition for each.
Notice that one of the words is used as a slang word in the play, so you will need to find the slang meaning of the word.

3.1) curtly – _____

3.2) haymaker (slang) – _____

3.3) serenely – _____

3.4) imperiously – _____

3.5) asperity – _____

3.6) chivalrous – _____

Check   **Correct**   **Recheck**

📖 **Read Act I, Scenes v-vi of**
The Miracle Worker.

- Scene v – in Annie's room
  - ☞ Begin your reading with, *"Meanwhile, inside,* ANNIE *has given* HELEN *a key; while* ANNIE *removes her bonnet,* HELEN *unlocks and opens the suitcase."*
- Scene vi – the Keller's living room and outdoors
  - ☞ End your reading at the end of Act I.

Helen Keller with horse

Review

Write the correct answers about Act I, Scenes v–vi.

3.7) How does Helen first behave toward Annie when they are in Annie's room? _____

_____

_____

_____

_____

3.8) How does James act? _____

_____

_____

3.9) Who are the antagonists in this part of Act I? How do they oppose the protagonist?

a. _____

_____

b. _____

_____

3.10) Reread the flashback Annie experiences while locked in her bedroom. What emotions do you think she feels? _____

_____

3.11) Why do you think Annie continues to hear the words "forever and ever" in her flashbacks?

_____

_____

3.12) In Annie's flashback, what do you think the doctor means when he says that her brother will be "going on a (journey)"? _____

_____

3.13) How does Annie feel toward Helen at the end of Act I? What does her reaction to Helen reveal about her? _____

_____

_____

3.14) Give an example of dramatic irony from this part of Act I. _____

_____

Explain the meaning of each idiom from Act I. If you need to, look up the meaning of the idiom on the Internet.

3.15) HELEN *is now in a rage, **fighting tooth and nail** to get out of the chair, and ANNIE answers while struggling and dodging her kicks.*

fighting tooth and nail – _____

3.16) KELLER [AT THE DOOR]: No need to shout, I've been **cooling my heels** for an hour. Sit down.

cooling my heels – _____

Check　　　Correct　　　Recheck

POINT OF VIEW

Since dramas are meant to be watched, the point of view is usually third-person objective. The audience views the actions onstage from an objective viewpoint, not from the perspective of any one character. In contrast, Helen Keller's autobiography is written from her personal perspective. She tells about events as she remembers them.

The following selection is from Helen Keller's autobiography, *The Story of My Life*. In Chapter IV, she tells about the time when Anne Sullivan first came to be her teacher. You read this part of the story in the drama; now you will read it from Helen's perspective.

Read the following selection. As you read, think about the similarities and differences between the autobiography and the play.

Chapter IV from *The Story of My Life*

by Helen Keller

The most important day I remember in all my life is the one on which my teacher, Anne Mansfield Sullivan, came to me. I am filled with wonder when I consider the immeasurable contrasts between the two lives which it connects. It was the third of March, 1887, three months before I was seven years old.

On the afternoon of that eventful day, I stood on the porch, dumb, expectant. I guessed vaguely from my mother's signs and from the hurrying to and fro in the house that something unusual was about to happen, so I went to the door and waited on the steps. The afternoon sun penetrated the mass of honeysuckle that covered the porch, and fell on my upturned face. My fingers lingered almost unconsciously on the familiar leaves and blossoms which had just come forth to greet the sweet southern spring. I did not know what the future held of marvel or surprise for me. Anger and bitterness had preyed upon me continually for weeks and a deep languor had succeeded this passionate struggle.

Have you ever been at sea in a dense fog, when it seemed as if a tangible white darkness shut you in, and the great ship, tense and anxious, groped her way toward the shore with plummet and sounding-line, and you waited with beating heart for something to happen? I was like that ship before my education began, only I was without compass or sounding-line, and had no way of knowing how near the harbor was. "Light! give me light!" was the wordless cry of my soul, and the light of love shone on me in that very hour.

Helen Keller at 8 years old
with her teacher Anne Sullivan

I felt approaching footsteps, I stretched out my hand as I supposed to my mother. Someone took it, and I was caught up and held close in the arms of her who had come to reveal all things to me, and, more than all things else, to love me.

The morning after my teacher came she led me into her room and gave me a doll. The little blind children at the Perkins Institution had sent it and Laura Bridgman had dressed it; but I did not know this until afterward. When I had played with it a little while, Miss Sullivan slowly spelled into my hand the word "d-o-l-l." I was at once interested in this finger play and tried to imitate it. When I finally succeeded in making the letters correctly I was flushed with childish pleasure and pride. Running downstairs to my mother I held up my hand and made the letters for doll. I did not know that I was spelling a word or even that words existed; I was simply making my fingers go in monkey-like imitation. In the days that followed I learned to spell in this uncomprehending way a great many words, among them pin, hat, cup and a few verbs like sit, stand and walk. But my teacher had been with me several weeks before I understood that everything has a name.

Review

Write the correct answers.

3.17) How is Helen Keller's account of her first day with Anne Sullivan different from the account presented in the drama? Consider that Helen wrote her autobiography about fifteen years after this event occurred. _____

_____

_____

3.18) Give an example of imagery from the second paragraph of the selection. _____

_____

_____

3.19) Explain the following sentence from the selection: "Anger and bitterness had preyed upon me continually for weeks and a deep languor had succeeded this passionate struggle."

_____

_____

_____

3.20) To what does Helen compare her life before Anne came to teach her and what does the comparison reveal about Helen? _____

_____

_____

Check   Correct   Recheck

(Each answer, 4 points)
Match the words to the descriptions.

1.01) _____ amiably

1.02) _____ facetiously

1.03) _____ asylum

1.04) _____ placating

1.05) _____ obstinate

1.06) _____ precocious

1.07) _____ spinster

1.08) _____ sotto voce

1.09) _____ asperity

1.010) _____ chivalrous

A. harshness; severity

B. advanced or mature in development

C. in a soft voice, so as not to be overheard

D. courteous; gracious; considerate

E. good-naturedly; pleasantly

F. stubborn; unyielding

G. conceding; pacifying

H. sarcastically; humorously

I. an institution for the care of the mentally ill or those requiring special assistance

J. an unmarried woman who is beyond usual marrying age

Choose the correct answers.

1.011) _____ What makes a drama different from prose writing?
A. Prose stories have setting and conflict, while dramas do not.
B. Prose stories use description to tell about characters' actions, while dramas use stage directions and are meant to be performed for an audience.
C. Prose stories do not have protagonists and antagonists, while dramas do.
D. Dramas use dialogue, while prose stories do not.

1.012) _____ In the drama, flashback scenes serve the purpose of ___.
A. giving information about Annie's past
B. reminding Annie of her inner sadness and regret
C. showing that Annie is still holding on to her past
D. all of these

1.013) _____ Which of the following is an example of an idiom?
    A. My love is like a red, red rose.
    B. Mr. Anagnos says Helen is "like a little safe, locked, that no one can open."
    C. It's raining cats and dogs outside.
    D. Helen Keller said her life was like a ship caught in a dense fog before she met Anne Sullivan.

1.014) _____ Who is the protagonist of the play?
    A. Helen Keller   B. Annie Sullivan   C. Kate Keller   D. James Keller

1.015) _____ Who is the strongest antagonist in the play?
    A. Helen Keller   C. Jimmie Sullivan
    B. Mr. Anagnos   D. Annie Sullivan

1.016) _____ Which of the following is an example of dramatic irony?
    A. At the beginning of Act I, the doctor says that Helen will fully recover from her illness.
    B. Helen pins Martha to the ground and takes her scissors.
    C. Helen overturns Mildred's cradle and puts her doll in it.
    D. Annie says that she will put one of the children in her suitcase to take to Alabama with her.

1.017) _____ The reader/audience gets a clear picture of what Helen is like through ___.
    A. Helen's own spoken words
    B. stage directions explaining Helen's actions
    C. Annie's letters describing Helen
    D. James's interactions with Helen

1.018) _____ What do Helen Keller and Laura Bridgman have in common?
    A. They were both instructed by Mr. Anagnos.
    B. They were both taught sign language by Annie Sullivan.
    C. They both graduated from Radcliffe College.
    D. They were both struck with illness at a young age and became deaf-blind.

1.019) _____ What is the genre of *The Miracle Worker*?
    A. comedy drama   C. historical drama
    B. tragedy drama   D. informational text

1.020) _____ What characteristic does Annie display in her reaction to Helen throwing the key into the well at the end of Act I?
    A. determination   C. rage
    B. despair   D. indifference

Identify the character who spoke each piece of dialogue using names from the box below.

> Helen Keller   Kate Keller   Captain Keller   James Keller
> Aunt Ev   Mr. Anagnos   Annie Sullivan

1.021) _____ Here's a houseful of grownups can't cope with the child, how can an inexperienced half-blind Yankee schoolgirl manage her?

1.022) _____ So. You are no longer our pupil, we throw you into the world, a teacher. If the child can be taught. No one expects you to work miracles, even for twenty-five dollars a month.

1.023) _____ Oh, you should have seen me when I left Boston. I got much older on this trip.

1.024) _____ You think she knows what she's doing? She imitates everything, she's a monkey.

1.025) _____ We can't get through to teach her to sit still. You are young, despite your years, to have such—confidence. Do you, inside?

Check   **Correct**   **Recheck**

4. ACT II, SCENES i–ii

Objectives:

- Read with fluency and comprehension.
- Use a dictionary or thesaurus to determine the meanings of words.
- Analyze how playwrights characterize their protagonists and antagonists through the dialogue and staging of their plays.
- Analyze how the central characters' qualities influence the theme of a fictional work and resolution of the central conflict.
- Use context to determine or clarify the meanings of unfamiliar words.
- Explain how the values and beliefs of particular characters are affected by the historical and cultural setting of the literary work.

BEGINNING ACT II

At the end of Act I, Annie begins to realize just what she is up against. Not only is Helen wild and unruly, she is crafty as well. Even though Helen cannot understand and communicate using language, Annie has hope that she can teach Helen. Annie recognizes that teaching such a strong-willed girl will be a challenge, but, being stubborn herself, Annie accepts this challenge. Helen's family, however, still does not believe that Helen is capable of learning language. As you read Act II of *The Miracle Worker*, be aware of instances in which Annie's ideas clash with the ideas of Helen's parents.

Anne Sullivan

PRE-READING VOCABULARY

Use the context clues in the sentence to determine the meaning of each bold word by choosing the correct definition or supplying a definition based on the context of the sentence.

4.1) HELEN *in her customary **unkempt** state is tucking her doll in the bottom drawer as a cradle, the contents of which she has dumped out, creating as usual a fine disorder.*

unkempt – _____

4.2) _____ ANNIE *alone in her room picks up things and in the act of removing* HELEN'S *doll gives way to unmannerly temptation: she **throttles** it.*
　　　　A. hugs　　　　B. stares at　　　　C. dresses　　　　D. strangles

4.3) KELLER: She's a *hireling*! Now I want it clear, unless there's an apology and complete change of manner she goes back on the next train!

hireling – _____

Look up the words in a dictionary and write a definition for each.

4.4) inarticulate – _____

4.5) proffered – _____

4.6) ominous – _____

4.7) deferential – _____

4.8) nincompoop – _____

4.9) nonplussed – _____

Check   Correct   Recheck

📖 **Read Act II, Scenes i–ii of *The Miracle Worker*.**
- Scene i – Annie's room
  - ☞ Begin reading at the beginning of Act II.
- Scene ii – in the dining room at breakfast the next morning

☞ End your reading with, "JAMES *stalks out, much offended, and* KATE *turning stares across the yard at the house; the lights narrowing down to the following pantomime in the family room leave her motionless in the dark.*"

Review

Answer the questions about Act II, Scenes i–ii.

4.10) What conflicts does Annie face in Scenes i–ii? _____

_____

_____

_____

_____

4.11) How does she respond to these conflicts? _____

_____

4.12) How does Kate respond when Helen stabs Annie's hand with a needle? _____

_____

4.13) James and Captain Keller discuss the Civil War Battle of Vicksburg, in which the Union General Grant and his army attacked Vicksburg for more than forty days and finally won. Vicksburg is considered a turning point in the war. What can you infer about the historical setting, based on their conversation? What opinions and political beliefs do they express?

_____

_____

_____

_____

4.14) Make inferences about Annie based on her interactions with the Kellers at breakfast. What characteristics does she display? How are her words and actions surprising? _____

_____

_____

_____

_____

4.15) What is Captain Keller of "half a mind" to do, and what does he want his wife to make "quite clear" to Annie? _____

_____

_____

Check   **Correct**   **Recheck**

The playwright of *The Miracle Worker*, William Gibson, got his idea for the play while reading Anne Sullivan's letters. She wrote many letters telling about events that occurred at the Keller house. The following letter was written a few days after Anne started teaching Helen. Compare Anne's personal account with the dramatic representation of the event you read about in *The Miracle Worker*.

Monday p.m.

I had a battle royal with Helen this morning. Although I try very hard not to force issues, I find it very difficult to avoid them.

Helen's table manners are appalling. She puts her hands in our plates and helps herself, and when the dishes are passed, she grabs them and takes out whatever she wants. This morning I would not let her put her hand in my plate. She persisted, and a contest of wills followed. Naturally the family was much disturbed, and left the room. I locked the dining-room door, and proceeded to eat my breakfast, though the food almost choked me. Helen was lying on the floor, kicking and screaming and trying to pull my chair from under me. She kept this up for half an hour, then she got up to see what I was doing. I let her see that I was eating, but did not let her put her hand in the plate. She pinched me, and I slapped her every time she did it. Then she went all round the table to see who was there, and finding no one but me, she seemed bewildered. After a few minutes she came back to her place and began to eat her breakfast with her fingers. I gave her a spoon, which she threw on the floor. I forced her out of the chair and made her pick it up. Finally I succeeded in getting her back in her chair again, and held the spoon in her hand, compelling her to take up the food with it and put it in her mouth. In a few minutes she yielded and finished her breakfast peaceably. Then we had another tussle over folding her napkin. When she had finished, she threw it on the floor and ran toward the door. Finding it locked, she began to kick and scream all over again. It was another hour before I succeeded in getting her napkin folded. Then I let her out into the warm sunshine and went up to my room and threw myself on the bed exhausted. I had a good cry and felt better. I suppose I shall have many such battles with the little woman before she learns the only two essential things I can teach her, obedience and love.

Review

Answer the questions about the letter.

4.16) What is one difference between Anne's account of the events and the description of events through the stage directions and dialogue in *The Miracle Worker*? _____

_____

_____

_____

4.17) Which one do you think was easier to understand—the letter or the play? _____

Why? _____

_____

4.18) What is the effect of the point of view of the letter? _____

_____

_____

Check   Correct   Recheck

Explain and make inferences based on the following quotations. What does each quotation tell you about the person who said it or the person to whom it was spoken? Do you agree or disagree with the quotation?

4.19) Annie: "The more I think the more I am certain that obedience is the gateway through

which knowledge enters the mind of the child." _____

_____

_____

4.20) Kate: "We catch our flies with honey, I'm afraid. We haven't the heart for much else, and so

many times she simply cannot be compelled." _____

_____

_____

4.21) Annie: "I'll tell you what I pity, that the sun won't rise and set for her all her life, and every

day you're telling her it will, what good will your pity do her when you're under the

strawberries, Captain Keller?" _____

_____

_____

4.22) Annie: "It's less trouble to feel sorry for her than teach her anything better, isn't it?"

_____

_____

_____

Reflection Question. Write your answer in complete sentences.

4.23) From what you have seen of Helen so far in the play, do you think she is acting like any normal child would act, or is she encouraged to act this way by those who reward her bad behavior? Explain your answer by referring to specific examples from the play.

_____

_____

_____

_____

_____

_____

Teacher Check ☐

5. ACT II, SCENES iii–iv

Objectives:

- Read with fluency and comprehension.

- Understand, make inferences, and draw conclusions about the structure and elements of drama and provide evidence from the text to support understanding.

- Use a dictionary or thesaurus to determine the meanings of words.

- Analyze how playwrights characterize their protagonists and antagonists through the dialogue and staging of their plays.

- Analyze how the central characters' qualities influence the theme of a fictional work and resolution of the central conflict.

Helen Keller

CONFLICT IN *THE MIRACLE WORKER*

As you read the end of Act I and the first two scenes of Act II, you probably noticed the tension beginning to build, between Annie and Helen, as well as between Annie and the Keller family. The Kellers disagree with the way Annie insists on working with Helen. Rather than indulge Helen's tantrums, Annie tries to teach Helen to communicate. So far, she has been unsuccessful, and Captain Keller intends to fire Annie because he believes she is doing more harm than good.

As you read the next section of Act II, the action will continue to increase.

Act II, Scene iii takes place after Annie orders the Keller family to leave the dining room. Helen is left alone with Annie in the room. In this scene, there is very little dialogue, as Helen is unable to hear and understand Annie's speech. Instead, Annie attempts to communicate with Helen through her actions. Pay close attention to the stage directions as you read, and try to imagine the action as it is described in the script. Think about how you would deal with Helen if you were in Annie's situation.

PRE-READING VOCABULARY
Look up the words in a dictionary and write a definition for each.

5.1) deftly – _____

5.2) compunction – _____

5.3) glower – _____

5.4) stolid – _____

5.5) disinter – _____

Check   Correct   Recheck

📖 **Read Act II, Scenes iii–iv of *The Miracle Worker*.**

- Scene iii – Annie and Helen in the dining room alone
  - ☞ Begin your reading with, "ANNIE *meanwhile has begun by slapping both keys down on a shelf out of* HELEN'S *reach; she returns to the table, upstage.*"
- Scene iv – outside the Keller house; Annie's room

☞ End your reading with, "ANNIE *gets to her feet. She drops the book on the bed, and pauses over her suitcase; after a moment she unclasps and opens it. Standing before it, she comes to her decision; she at once turns to the bureau, and taking her things out of its drawers, commences to throw them into the open suitcase.*"

Write the correct answers about Act II, Scenes iii–iv.

5.6) Describe the series of conflicts that Annie and Helen engage in at the breakfast table.

_____

_____

_____

_____

_____

5.7) What happens after the "pregnant moment"? (Note: In this context, *pregnant* means "highly significant.") Is this the end of Annie's troubles with Helen? Explain. _____

_____

_____

5.8) How does Annie respond to Helen's tantrums and violence? Do you think her actions were necessary, or were they too harsh? Explain your answer._____

_____

_____

_____

5.9) Does Annie succeed in resolving the conflict with Helen? Which character qualities does Annie display? _____

_____

5.10) What comparison does the playwright use to describe Helen as she exits the house to find her mother? How does this description give you more insight into what happened in the dining room? _____

_____

_____

5.11) What does Helen do that astonishes Kate? _____

5.12) In Scene iv, Annie goes up to her room and reads a book, the report from the Perkins Institute that she brought with her. Make an inference—whose voice does Annie hear reading the report, and who is the woman described in the report? _____

_____

5.13) Describe the flashback Annie experiences while reading the report. _____

_____

_____

_____

_____

5.14) What "goes into Annie like a sword"? What does this comparison tell you about her

feelings about the memory? _____

_____

5.15) What does it seem that Annie is doing at the end of today's reading—Act II, Scene iv?

What do you think will happen? _____

_____

Check   Correct   Recheck

THE ROLE OF FLASHBACKS

From your reading and research, you know that Anne Sullivan had a little brother, Jimmie, with whom she was very close. They both go to live at the almshouse in Tewksbury, Massachusetts, after their mother died and their father left them. Anne promises to take care of Jimmie, but due to the poor living conditions at the almshouse, Jimmie died at a young age. The vivid memories of her unfortunate childhood and the event of Jimmie's death continue to haunt Anne while she is at the Keller homestead. Flashbacks in the play give the audience insight into Anne's emotional conflicts, as she struggles with letting go of her past. The internal conflicts Anne faces only heighten her external conflicts with Helen and the rest of the Keller family.

Think about a vivid memory that you have, perhaps one from your childhood, that continues

Anne Sullivan

to affect you to this day. The memory does not have to be a sad one, but it should be one that evokes some kind of emotion. What does the memory reveal about your past? How do you feel when you recall the memory today? Why is the memory so important to you?

ACTIVITY: FLASHBACK

5.16) On your own paper, write your memory in the form of a "flashback scene" in a drama. Include a list of characters and descriptions, dialogue, and stage directions, and write it in the form of a script. Review the flashback scenes from Act I and Act II for examples. Your flashback scene should be at least ¾-page in length.

 **Teacher Check**

6. ACT II, SCENES v–vii

Objectives:

- Read with fluency and comprehension.
- Understand, make inferences, and draw conclusions about the structure and elements of drama and provide evidence from the text to support understanding.
- Use a dictionary or thesaurus to determine the meanings of words.
- Analyze how playwrights characterize their protagonists and antagonists through the dialogue and staging of their plays.
- Analyze how the central characters' qualities influence the theme of a fictional work and resolution of the central conflict.

In Scenes iii–iv of Act II, you saw the highest point of conflict between Annie and Helen. Annie won the battle at the breakfast table, but she has not yet won the war. Annie has not succeeded in winning Helen over so that she can teach her. At the end of Scene iv, Annie begins packing her suitcase. She must make a decision about what to do next. Unbeknownst to Annie, Captain Keller is also trying to make a decision about whether to allow Annie to continue teaching Helen. He feels that Annie has caused more damage and has made all of their lives more difficult. The next three scenes of Act II will show the outcomes of these decisions.

PRE-READING VOCABULARY

Look up the words in a dictionary and write a definition for each.

6.1) frivolous – _____

6.2) dourly – _____

6.3) irate – _____

6.4) quizzically – _____

6.5) imp – _____

6.6) paroxysm – _____

6.7) contempt – _____

Check   Correct   Recheck

📖 **Read Act II, Scenes v-vii of *The Miracle Worker*.**

- Scene v – at the Keller's garden house
  - ☞ Begin reading with, *"In the darkness down left a hand strikes a match, and lights a hanging oil lamp. It is KELLER'S hand, and his voice* accompanies it, very angry . . ."
- Scene vi – in the living room
- Scene vii – at the garden house
  - ☞ Read to the end of Act II.

Review

Write the correct answers about Act ii, Scenes v–vii.

6.8) At the beginning of Scene v, how does Captain Keller judge Annie's success? Does he feel she has been successful with Helen? Why or why not? _____

_____

_____

6.9) What is Kate's response to Captain Keller's judgment of Annie? _____

_____

_____

6.10) Make inferences about the interaction between Annie and Captain Keller in the garden house. How does each person behave? Who seems to be in control of the conversation?

_____

_____

_____

6.11) Describe the conditions under which Annie grew up, according to her own testimony. What effect did living at the almshouse have on her? _____

_____

_____

_____

6.12) What plan does Annie devise to teach Helen to depend on her? _____

_____

_____

_____

6.13) What metaphor does Annie use to describe her plan? (Hint: "All's fair in love and war.")

_____

6.14) What can you infer about Captain Keller's response to Annie's question about whether he likes Helen? _____

_____

6.15) How does the playwright indicate the passing of time that occurs after the Kellers leave the garden house and before James comes to talk to Annie? _____

_____

_____

6.16) How does James act as an antagonist toward Annie in Scene v? _____

_____

_____

6.17) How does Helen react to her "new" surroundings? What simile and metaphor are used to describe her? _____

_____

_____

_____

6.18) What can you infer is the reason behind James's attitude toward his father? _____

_____

_____

6.19) How does Annie respond when she hears Jimmie's voice in Scene vii? _____

_____

_____

6.20) How does Annie get Helen to let her touch her? _____

_____

6.21) Describe the mood at the end of Act II. _____

_____

Check   Correct   Recheck

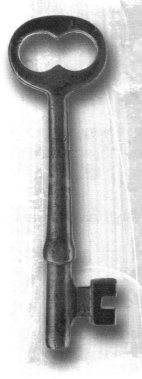

FIVE KEYS TO INITIATIVE

1 – **Look for Needs**: A person who has initiative understands his or her surroundings and completes the small details without being asked. Know what is going on around you so that you can address the needs you find.

2 – **Seize the Moment**: You may dream of greatness, but if you do not make the most of today's opportunities, your dreams will never become reality. As Benjamin Franklin said, "One today is worth two tomorrows." When you see something you should do—start today!

3 – **Make the Team Successful**: Do not assume that someone else will take care of needs you see. Bring it to the attention of your leaders, or address it yourself. In the process, make certain that you do not neglect your responsibilities or interfere with others' responsibilities.

4 – **Think Ahead**: Think through a project or event so that you can have everything you need at the right time. Anticipate what problems may arise, and try to prevent them.

5 – **Spend Time Wisely**: Often, people get into trouble because they are idle. Instead of finding something productive to do, they find mischief. Spend time wisely by reading a book, studying ahead, cleaning up, or volunteering to help someone else.

(Each answer, 5 points)
Choose the correct answers.

2.01) _____ After Helen stabs Annie with a sewing needle, what does Kate do that makes Annie angry?
  A. She slaps Helen's wrist.
  B. She won't let Helen eat dinner.
  C. She gives Helen a toy.
  D. She gives Helen a piece of candy.

2.02) _____ What statement by Captain Keller causes Annie to lose her temper at breakfast?
  A. He calls Annie incompetent.
  B. He says that Annie needs to have pity for Helen.
  C. He says that Annie needs to be more firm with Helen.
  D. He calls her a blind Yankee.

2.03) _____ To what does the playwright compare Helen as she exits the house after her fight with Annie in the dining room?
  A. a sad puppy
  B. a sly crocodile
  C. a ruined bat out of hell
  D. a busy bee

2.04) _____ What does Helen do at the breakfast table that amazes Kate?
  A. She counts to ten.
  B. She folds her napkin.
  C. She drinks all her milk.
  D. She jumps on top of the table and stomps on it.

2.05) _____ What do the "crones" in Annie's flashback tell her not to do?
  A. They tell her not to tell anyone where she came from.
  B. They tell her not to go to the school for the blind.
  C. They tell her not to cry about her brother dying.
  D. They tell her not to play in the deadhouse.

2.06) _____ Why does Annie ask for permission for Helen to live in the garden house alone with her for two weeks?
  A. Annie wants Helen to be completely dependent on her.
  B. Annie cannot teach a child who continually runs away.
  C. Annie does not want Helen to run to her parents who give her everything she wants.
  D. all of these

2.07) _____ Which of the following does NOT describe the asylum where Annie grew up?
  A. It was filled with rats.
  B. Most of the babies born there lived.
  C. Children could play in the deadhouse where they kept dead bodies until graves were dug.
  D. Many of the people who lived there were diseased and dying.

2.08) _____ How does James act as an antagonist to Annie?
   A. He tells her that Helen hates her.
   B. He calls Annie names.
   C. He tells Annie that she will never succeed, so she should just give up.
   D. He physically abuses Annie.

2.09) _____ Whose help does Annie enlist to get Helen to let Annie touch her again?
   A. Percy's   B. Martha's   C. Kate's   D. James'

Match the words with the descriptions.

2.010) _____ nonplussed

2.011) _____ compunction

2.012) _____ glower

2.013) _____ paroxysm

2.014) _____ nincompoop

2.015) _____ contempt

A. a foolish person

B. perplexed, confused

C. a violent outburst

D. a feeling of disdain or scorn

E. an expression of dislike or anger

F. a feeling of uneasiness or remorse

Fill in the blanks using words from the box below.

| unkempt | inarticulate | deftly | irate | imp |

2.016) Because Bob had stuffed half of a burger in his mouth, he was _____ and had to grunt and use hand signals to tell his sister that there was an enormous bug crawling around in her hair.

2.017) When Ronnie tried to sneak into his sister's room to listen in on her phone conversation with her boyfriend, she spied him and yelled, "You little _____! Get out of my room!"

2.018) Destiny plays the piano very _____, and she has won many awards.

2.019) Martin comes to school every day with _____ hair; it always looks like he has just rolled out of bed.

2.020) Rowan became _____ when he came home to find his most expensive pair of shoes, chewed to pieces and scattered all over the living room.

Check   Correct   Recheck

7. ACT III, SCENES i–iii

Objectives:

- Read with fluency and comprehension.
- Understand, make inferences, and draw conclusions about the structure and elements of drama and provide evidence from the text to support understanding.
- Use a dictionary or thesaurus to determine the meanings of words.
- Analyze how playwrights characterize their protagonists and antagonists through the dialogue and staging of their plays.
- Analyze linear plot developments to determine whether and how conflicts are resolved.
- Analyze different forms of point of view.
- Use context to determine or clarify the meanings of unfamiliar words.

PLOT IN *THE MIRACLE WORKER*

As you begin reading Act III, consider how the plot has developed throughout the drama so far. At the beginning of the play, the audience is introduced to the characters and the basic situation of the story. You discovered that Helen is deaf and blind due to an illness she had as a toddler. In the following scenes of Act I, you learned about Helen's family, her mother and father, James, Aunt Ev, and the Keller's servants, Viney, Martha, and Percy. You were also introduced to the character of Annie Sullivan. At the end of Act I, Annie arrives at the Keller homestead and begins working with Helen. At this point of the story, the major conflict is introduced, as Annie discovers just how difficult teaching Helen will be. The very last scene in Act I emphasizes Annie's confidence and her determination to teach Helen.

Act II is all about conflict between the characters. It seems that almost everyone is against Annie—Helen, Captain Keller, James Keller, and even Kate at times. The conflict heightens during the scene at the breakfast table when Annie and Helen fight over Helen's table manners. Annie seems to make progress with the Keller family, as she is able to convince

Helen Keller

them to allow Helen to stay with her alone at the garden house. However, the conflicts do not end as Helen continues to obstinately oppose Annie. In addition to the external conflicts in Act II, Annie still struggles with an internal conflict, as the flashbacks continue to remind her of the guilt she feels about her brother's death. At the end of Act II, the external conflict seems to be settling down, as the final scene shows Helen sleeping and Annie singing to her.

In the next two Lessons, you will be reading the final act of *The Miracle Worker*. So far, the conflicts have not been completely resolved. Captain and Mrs. Keller have not yet put their faith in Annie's teaching methods. Annie has not been successful in teaching Helen language. James and Captain Keller still have a very tense relationship. As you read Act III, look for ways in which these conflicts move toward their resolutions.

PRE-READING VOCABULARY

Use the context clues in the sentence to determine the meaning of each bold word by choosing the correct definition or supplying a definition based on the context of the sentence.

7.1) KATE: It's true. The two weeks have been normal, quiet, all you say. But not short. **Interminable**.

interminable – _____

7.2) _____ ANNIE, *haggard at the table, is writing a letter, her face again almost in contact with the stationery . . .* "I, feel, every, day, more, and, more, inadequate."

    A. cheerful   C. healthy

    B. looking worn and exhausted   D. strong

Look up the words in a dictionary and write a definition for each.

7.3) boon – _____

7.4) wistful – _____

7.5) withering – _____

7.6) forlorn – _____

Check   Correct   Recheck

📖 **Read Act III, Scenes i–iii of *The Miracle Worker*.**
- Scene i – at the garden house/inside the Keller house
- Scene ii – at the garden house
- Scene iii – the final hour at the garden house

☞End your reading with, "KELLER *smiles, offers his arm . . .* ANNIE *takes it, and the lights lose them as he escorts her out.*"

Write the correct answers about Act III, Scenes i–iii.

7.7) How does Annie feel at the beginning of Act III? _____

_____

7.8) How does Kate feel about Helen's absence? _____

7.9) How does James feel? _____

_____

7.10) What change in behavior does James show as he talks to Kate after breakfast? _____

_____

_____

7.11) What is the first obvious change that Kate observes in Helen while Helen is still at the

garden house? _____

7.12) What does Annie mean when she tells Kate, "We're born to use words, like wings, it has

to come"? _____

_____

7.13) What does Annie ask Kate for? _____

_____

7.14) What is Kate's response? _____

7.15) Are Kate and Captain Keller happy with Helen's progress? _____ How has Helen changed?

_____

7.16) Is Annie satisfied? _____ Why or why not? _____

_____

7.17) What does Helen begin doing to Belle when Belle is brought to her? _____

_____

7.18) What simile is used to describe how Annie feels as she leaves the garden house? _____

_____

_____

7.19) What does the simile indicate? _____

_____

7.20) As Annie is left alone in the garden house and begins to leave it, how does lighting indicate a change of mood? _____

_____

_____

7.21) In Act II, Annie makes the statement that "obedience is the gateway through which knowledge enters the mind of the child." In Act III, Annie says that "to do nothing but obey is—no gift, obedience without understanding is a—blindness, too." Explain how these quotations indicate a change in Annie's thinking, and explain what you think has caused the change.

_____

_____

_____

_____

7.22) What "lie" does Annie refer to as she speaks to Captain Keller? _____

_____

_____

7.23) How has Captain Keller's opinion of Annie changed? What has caused his change of opinion?

_____

_____

WORD ETYMOLOGY

The English word initiative came from the Latin verb *initiare*, which means "to begin; to originate."

ini•tia•tive *n.* 1: the power or ability to begin or to follow through with a plan or task; 2: a beginning or introductory step; an opening; 3: the lead

March 20, 1887

My heart is singing for joy this morning. A miracle has happened! The light of understanding has shone upon my little pupil's mind, and behold, all things are changed!

The wild little creature of two weeks ago has been transformed into a gentle child. She is sitting by me as I write, her face serene and happy, crocheting a long red chain of Scotch wool. She learned the stitch this week, and is very proud of the achievement. When she succeeded in making a chain that would reach across the room, she patted herself on the arm and put the first work of her hands lovingly against her cheek. She lets me kiss her now, and when she is in a particularly gentle mood, she will sit in my lap for a minute or two; but she does not return my caresses. The great step—the step that counts—has been taken. The little savage has learned her first lesson in obedience, and finds the yoke easy. It now remains my pleasant task to direct and mold the beautiful intelligence that is beginning to stir in the child-soul. Already people remark the change in Helen. Her father looks

Helen Keller

in at us morning and evening as he goes to and from his office, and sees her contentedly stringing her beads or making horizontal lines on her sewing-card, and exclaims, "How quiet she is!" When I came, her movements were so insistent that one always felt there was something unnatural and almost weird about her. I have noticed also that she eats much less, a fact which troubles her father so much that he is anxious to get her home. He says she is homesick. I don't agree with him; but I suppose we shall have to leave our little bower [cottage] very soon.

Helen has learned several nouns this week. "M-u-g" and "m-i-l-k," have given her more trouble than other words. When she spells "milk," she points to the mug, and when she spells "mug," she makes the sign for pouring or drinking, which shows that she has confused the words. She has no idea yet that everything has a name.

Yesterday I had the little Negro boy come in when Helen was having her lesson, and learn the letters, too. This pleased her very much and stimulated her ambition to excel Percy. She was delighted if he made a mistake, and made him form the letter over several times. When he succeeded in forming it to suit her, she patted him on his woolly head so vigorously that I thought some of his slips were intentional.

One day this week Captain Keller brought Belle, a setter of which he is very proud, to see us. He wondered if Helen would recognize her old playmate. Helen was giving Nancy a bath, and didn't notice the dog at first. She usually feels the softest step and throws out her arms to ascertain if anyone is near her. Belle didn't seem very anxious to attract her attention. I imagine she has been rather roughly handled sometimes by her little mistress. The dog hadn't been in the room more than half a minute, however, before Helen began to sniff, and dumped the doll into the wash-bowl and felt about the room. She stumbled upon Belle, who was crouching near the window where Captain Keller was standing. It was evident that she recognized the dog; for she put her arms round her neck and squeezed her. Then Helen sat down by her and began to manipulate her claws. We couldn't think for a second what she was doing; but when we saw her make the letters "d-o-l-l" on her own fingers, we knew that she was trying to teach Belle to spell.

Answer the questions about the letter.

7.24) What three events did the playwright of *The Miracle Worker* draw on as referred to in Annie's letter?

a. _____

b. _____

c. _____

7.25) How does the point of view of the letter affect your understanding of the events? _____

_____

_____

7.26) Which genre is easier to understand—the letter or the drama? _____

Which one do you prefer and why? _____

_____

Check   **Correct**   **Recheck**

8. ACT III, SCENES iv–v

Objectives:

- Read with fluency and comprehension.
- Understand, make inferences, and draw conclusions about the structure and elements of drama and provide evidence from the text to support understanding.
- Understand, make inferences, and draw conclusions about the structure and elements of fiction and provide evidence from text to support understanding.
- Analyze how playwrights characterize their protagonists and antagonists through the dialogue and staging of their plays.
- Analyze how the central characters' qualities influence the theme of a fictional work and resolution of the central conflict.
- Analyze linear plot developments to determine whether and how conflicts are resolved.
- Analyze different forms of point of view.

In Lesson 8, you will complete your reading of *The Miracle Worker*. As you read the remainder of Act III, pay attention to how conflict continues to drive the action to the end of the story. Also, think about how conflicts are resolved as a result of changes characters undergo.

📖 **Read Act III, Scenes iv–v of *The Miracle Worker*.**

- Scene iv – in the dining room
  - ☞ Begin your reading with, *"Now in the family room the rear door opens, and* HELEN *steps in. She stands a moment, then sniffs in one deep grateful breath, and her hands go out vigorously to familiar things . . ."*
- Scene v – outside at the water pump
  - ☞ Read until the end of Act III.

Review

Write the correct answers about Act III, Scenes iv–v.

8.1) What does Helen do to "test" Annie and her family? _____

_____

_____

8.2) How does Annie respond? _____

_____

8.3) How do Captain Keller and Kate respond? _____

_____

8.4) Describe the conflict that ensues between Captain Keller and Annie. _____

_____

_____

_____

8.5) How does James stand up for Annie? _____

_____

8.6) What does this action tell you about him? _____

_____

8.7) Describe what happens at the water pump. _____

_____

_____

_____

8.8) What word does Helen first communicate to her mother? _____

8.9) What can you infer from this action? _____

_____

8.10) What does Helen give to Annie at the end of the play and why is this significant? _____

_____

8.11) What words does Annie spell into Helen's hand and whisper to her at the end of the play?

_____

8.12) What is the significance of Annie's final words in the play? How does her statement signify
a change? Think about her flashbacks and the voices she has been hearing. Why does
Annie stop hearing voices? How do lighting and color emphasize the change? _____

_____

_____

_____

_____

Check   **Correct**   **Recheck**

Read the letter written by Anne Sullivan about the event portrayed in Act III of the drama.

April 5, 1887

I must write you a line this morning because something very important has happened. Helen has taken the second great step in her education. She has learned that EVERYTHING HAS A NAME, AND THAT THE MANUAL ALPHABET IS THE KEY TO EVERYTHING SHE WANTS TO KNOW.

In a previous letter I think I wrote you that "mug" and "milk" had given Helen  more trouble than all the rest. She confused the nouns with the verb "drink." She didn't know the word for "drink," but went through the pantomime of drinking whenever she spelled "mug" or "milk." This morning, while she was washing, she wanted to know the name for "water." When she wants to know the name of anything, she points to it and pats my hand. I spelled "w-a-t-e-r" and thought no more about it until after breakfast. Then it occurred to me that with the help of this new word I might succeed in straightening out the "mug-milk" difficulty. We went out to the pump-house, and I made Helen hold her mug under the spout while I pumped. As the cold water gushed forth, filling the mug, I spelled "w-a-t-e-r" in Helen's free hand. The word coming so close upon the sensation of cold water rushing over her hand seemed to startle her. She dropped the mug and stood as one transfixed. A new light came into her face. She spelled "water" several times. Then she dropped on the ground and asked for its name and pointed to the pump and the trellis, and suddenly turning round she asked for my name. I spelled "Teacher." Just then the nurse brought Helen's little sister into the pump-house, and Helen spelled "baby" and pointed to the nurse. All the way back to the house she was highly excited, and learned the name of every object she touched, so that in a few hours she had added thirty new words to her vocabulary. Here are some of them: DOOR, OPEN, SHUT, GIVE, GO, COME, and a great many more.

P.S.—I didn't finish my letter in time to get it posted last night; so I shall add a line. Helen got up this morning like a radiant fairy. She has flitted from object to object, asking the name of everything and kissing me for very gladness. Last night when I got in bed, she stole into my arms of her own accord and kissed me for the first time, and I thought my heart would burst, so full was it of joy.

Answer the questions.

8.13) How does Anne's account in her letter differ from the final scene of the play? _____

_____

_____

_____

8.14) How does Anne describe Helen's reaction to learning her first word? _____

_____

_____

8.15) Which one, the letter or the play, captures the emotion of the scene more effectively?

Explain your answer. _____

_____

PLOT AND CONFLICT RESOLUTION

Now that you have read the entire play, you can see that the conflict continues to drive the story all the way to the end. In the past you have charted the plot of a story using a triangle plot diagram. However, *The Miracle Worker* does not follow the typical plot triangle. Instead, the conflict and emotion continue to build until they reach a peak at the end of the play. It is not until the last few pages of the drama that Annie finally achieves the breakthrough with Helen that she has been striving for almost since the beginning of the play.

Consider how conflicts are resolved at the end of the drama. Some conflicts, such as the one between James and Kate, are resolved before the end of the play, but the major ones do not come to a resolution until the very end. In some cases, the resolution of a conflict is implied, not expressly stated or described. Think about how external as well as internal conflicts are resolved.

CHARACTER DEVELOPMENT

Most of the characters in *The Miracle Worker* change from the beginning of the play to the end, and many of them change in more than one way. You have already seen one way that Annie shows change at the end of the story. Has she changed in other ways as well? As you examine characters, consider how they have developed in their attitudes, actions, and thoughts.

Answer the questions.

8.16) What event makes up the climax of the play, the highest point of action or emotion?

_____

8.17) Why do you think the playwright chose to end the play the way he did, at its emotional peak?

_____

_____

Describe the outcome of each of the conflicts.

8.18) Annie's internal conflict, experiencing guilt over her brother's death: _____

_____

_____

8.19) Annie's conflict with Helen: _____

_____

8.20) Captain Keller's conflict with Annie: _____

_____

8.21) James's conflict with Captain Keller: _____

_____

8.22) Helen's internal conflict, learning and understanding language: _____

_____

_____

Describe the changes that occur in each of the characters, including how each was influenced by Annie. Consider how Annie's character qualities influenced the change.

8.23) Kate Keller – _____

_____

8.24) Captain Keller – _____

_____

8.25) James Keller – _____

_____

8.26) Which characters do not change throughout the story? If you need to, consult the cast list at the beginning of the play.

a. _____   d. _____

b. _____   e. _____

c. _____

Check   Correct   Recheck

8.27) Which character do you think changed most throughout the play? Explain what that character was like at the beginning of the play, and describe the changes he or she has undergone, including what causes each change. Support your answer using quotations and describing specific scenes from the play. Your answer should be at least one complete, well-written paragraph in length.

_____

_____

_____

_____

_____

_____

_____

_____

_____

_____

_____

_____

_____

_____

_____

_____

_____

Teacher Check

9. THEME IN *THE MIRACLE WORKER*

Objectives:

- Analyze how playwrights characterize their protagonists and antagonists through the dialogue and staging of their plays.
- Analyze how the central characters' qualities influence the theme of a fictional work and resolution of the central conflict.
- Write responses to literary texts that demonstrate the use of writing skills for a multi-paragraph essay and provide sustained evidence from the text using quotations when appropriate.

Vocabulary:

theme – the central truth or message presented through a work of literature

THEME

As you have learned in other Units this year, the **theme** of a work is the central message or truth presented through a work of literature. Now that you have completed *The Miracle Worker*, think about what truths or messages the playwright has communicated through this work. Remember, works of literature can have multiple themes. You can determine themes in a literary work by examining how characters (especially the central character) change throughout the work, how conflicts are resolved, and how the work emphasizes certain concepts through the words and actions of the main characters.

Think about how the main characters change throughout *The Miracle Worker*. The most obvious change takes place in Helen Keller, as she understands the importance of language and learns to trust her teacher, Annie Sullivan. Annie changes throughout the novel by overcoming many obstacles, such as Helen's stubbornness, Captain Keller's lack of confidence in her abilities, her own inability to let go of the past, and discouragement from James Keller. Annie's response to each of these obstacles shows her character, which reflects the theme of the work.

At the end of the story, the main conflicts reach a resolution. Annie finally succeeds in teaching Helen about language and meaning, and Captain and Mrs. Keller see the results of Annie's hard work. James stands up to his father in Annie's defense and shows a change of character by advocating for Helen's best interest. In the final dramatic scene of the play, Annie learns to love Helen and releases the memories of her painful past.

THEMES IN *THE MIRACLE WORKER*

The following themes are present in *The Miracle Worker*. These are not the only themes in the play, but each one is a prominent message reflected in the story.

1 – Communication is necessary for human relationships.

Helen's major problem is her inability to communicate. She cannot see, hear, or speak, and the only way she knows how to express herself is through temper tantrums. Her family members do not know how to reach her; therefore, she does not experience a *real* relationship with any of them. Each of her family members responds in a different way to Helen, but none of them treat her as a human being. Helen's mother indulges all of Helen's tantrums and gives her whatever will pacify her. Captain Keller wants to confine Helen because he thinks she is a menace to the rest of the family. James ignores Helen as much as he can. He thinks she is stupid, and that teaching her is an impossible task. All of the Kellers basically treat Helen as they would a house pet; their primary concern is that Helen learn to obey.

Once Annie arrives, Helen experiences her first real human relationship. It is through Annie's diligence that Helen learns to communicate, and she learns to love and trust Annie. Annie knows that it is not enough to simply learn to behave and obey; Helen must understand language in order to experience relationships with other people. Once Helen is able to communicate, Annie learns to love again for the first time since her brother died.

2 – With determination and patience, one can overcome great difficulties.

Life for Annie has not been easy. From losing her mother and being abandoned by her father, to living in a rat-infested almshouse and experiencing the death of her brother, Annie's life has been marked by difficulty. Annie shows great determination by refusing to give up. She seeks out a school for the blind and convinces them to accept her. Once she begins teaching Helen, she does not even entertain the thought of giving up, even when others encourage her to do so. At the end of Act I, after Helen has locked Annie in her room and thrown the key down the well, Annie says, "You think I'm so easily gotten rid of? You have a thing or two to learn, first." Annie knows that in order to teach Helen how to communicate, she must be persistent and patient.

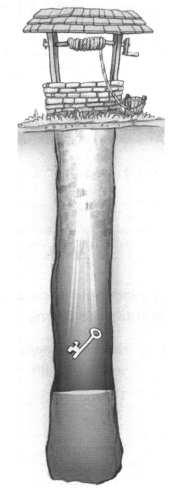

Annie's determination also enables her to stand up to Captain Keller on a few occasions. She knows what Helen needs, and she convinces Captain Keller to let her have control over Helen so that she can teach her effectively. Because of her determination, Annie is successful in teaching Helen the importance of language.

3 – The value of an individual must never be underestimated.

Helen's family members clearly do not know her true capabilities. They think that it is impossible to teach her language, and instead of trying to communicate with her and discipline her, they give her everything she wants. In Act III, Captain Keller shows that he does not believe his daughter can learn to communicate. When Helen tries to spell words on the dog's paws, Captain Keller states: "The dog doesn't know what she means, any more than she knows what you mean, Miss Sullivan. I think you ask too much, of her and yourself. God may not have meant Helen to have the—eyes you speak of." Captain Keller underestimates both Helen's ability to learn and Annie's ability to teach her.

At the end of the story, Helen's parents are amazed that she has actually understood that words have meaning. They did not believe Helen would ever grasp language. As you know, the end of the play is not the end of Helen's story. She went on to be a famous speaker, author, and civil rights activist. None of her accomplishments would have been possible had not one individual—Annie Sullivan—showed patience and perseverance in teaching Helen language and the importance of communication.

Review

Answer the question.

9.1) How can you determine the theme of a literary work? _____

_____

_____

_____

Explain how each of the quotations from the play reflects a theme discussed in this Lesson. Identify the theme, and describe how the quotation shows that theme.

9.2) KELLER: There are of course all kinds of separation, Katie has lived with one kind for five years. (Act III)

Theme: _____

_____

Describe: _____

_____

9.3) ANNIE: I grew up in such an asylum. The state almshouse. . . . No, it made me strong. (Act II)

Theme: _____

_____

Describe: _____

_____

9.4) KELLER: Here's a houseful of grownups can't cope with the child, how can an inexperienced half-blind Yankee schoolgirl manage her? (Act I)

Theme: _____

_____

Describe: _____

_____

9.5) ANNIE: Mrs. Keller, don't lose heart just because I'm not on my last legs. I have three big advantages over Dr. Howe that money couldn't buy for you. One is his work behind me . . . Another is to be young, why, I've got energy to do anything. The third is, I've been blind. (Act I)

Theme: _____

_____

Describe: _____

_____

9.6) JAMES: You think she knows what she's doing? She imitates everything, she's a monkey. (Act I)

Theme: _____

_____

Describe: _____

_____

9.7) ANNIE: Helen, Helen, the chick has to come out of its shell, sometime. You come out, too . . . There's only one way out, for you, and it's language. (Act III)

Theme: _____

_____

Describe: _____

_____

9.8) ANNIE: It's less trouble to feel sorry for her than to teach her anything better, isn't it?

Theme: _____

_____

Describe: _____

_____

ACTIVITY: THEME

Illustrate and explain a theme from *The Miracle Worker*.

Illustration:

9.9) Choose one of the three major themes from *The Miracle Worker* discussed in this Lesson. Then, consider the scene from the play that best portrays that theme. Draw a picture to illustrate that scene. Use a piece of plain white paper to draw your picture.

Essay:

9.10) On a separate sheet of paper, write or type an essay at least two paragraphs in length that explains how the theme is displayed throughout the entire play, and specifically in the scene you illustrated.
- The first paragraph should introduce and describe the theme. Also, discuss the overall significance of the theme in the play.
- The second paragraph should explain how the specific scene you illustrated best exemplifies the theme you chose. Use quotations and specific examples from the play to explain how the theme is portrayed in that scene.

Teacher Check

MY SCORE

TEACHER
INITIAL

(Each answer, 5 points)
Choose the correct answers.

3.01) _____ Which character is the most anxious to have Helen back at home?
     A. Captain Keller   C. James Keller
     B. Kate Keller   D. Annie Sullivan

3.02) _____ What observation does Kate make about Helen when she talks to Annie on the morning of Helen's return?
     A. She says that Helen looks happier.
     B. She is surprised that Helen has learned to talk.
     C. She thinks that Helen looks sad and lonely.
     D. She notices that Helen looks serene and behaves more politely.

3.03) _____ How does Annie feel about leaving the garden house?
     A. She feels relieved to be getting rid of Helen.
     B. She feels proud of her accomplishments with Helen.
     C. She feels like a failure because she was not able to teach Helen to communicate.
     D. She feels confident that Helen will continue to learn language in the real world.

3.04) _____ Annie says that "obedience without understanding is a ___."
     A. lie   B. blindness   C. gift   D. punishment

3.05) _____ When Helen returns home, what does she do to "test" Annie and her family?
     A. She repeatedly throws her napkin on the floor at the dinner table.
     B. She overturns Mildred's cradle.
     C. She refuses to eat any food.
     D. She locks Annie in her room.

3.06) _____ Who stands up for Annie to Captain Keller and defends her methods of teaching Helen?
     A. Kate Keller   B. James Keller   C. Viney   D. Percy

3.07) _____ What is Helen's first spoken word, according to the play?
     A. mother   B. Helen   C. water   D. baby

3.08) _____ What word does Helen first sign to her mother?
     A. love   B. mother   C. Helen   D. teacher

3.09) _____ What indicates the end of Annie's internal conflict at the end of the play?
- A. She stops hearing voices.
- B. The lighting changes.
- C. She begins to love Helen.
- D. all of these

3.010) _____ Which of the following characters does not change throughout the play?
- A. Aunt Ev
- B. James Keller
- C. Captain Keller
- D. Annie Sullivan

3.011) _____ What is the climax of *The Miracle Worker*?
- A. Helen throws a tantrum at her homecoming party.
- B. Kate and Captain Keller refuse to allow Annie another week of solitude with Helen.
- C. Helen says her first word and finally understands that words have meaning.
- D. Helen learns to crochet.

Identify the three themes from *The Miracle Worker* discussed in Lesson 9.

3.012) _____

_____

3.013) _____

_____

3.014) _____

_____

Match the words with the descriptions.

3.015) _____ interminable

3.016) _____ haggard

3.017) _____ boon

3.018) _____ wistful

3.019) _____ withering

3.020) _____ forlorn

- A. fading; losing strength
- B. unhappy
- C. never-ending
- D. a benefit or blessing
- E. longing; yearning
- F. having a worn or exhausted appearance

Check   **Correct**   **Recheck**

STOP and prepare for the Unit Practice Test.
- Review the Objectives and Vocabulary for each Lesson.
- Reread each Lesson and its corresponding questions.
- Relearn each Lesson that you still do not understand.
- Review the Quizzes.

PRACTICE TEST

(Each answer, 4 points)
Match the words with the descriptions.

1) _____ irate

2) _____ unkempt

3) _____ interminable

4) _____ nonplussed

5) _____ haggard

6) _____ forlorn

7) _____ inarticulate

8) _____ asylum

9) _____ facetiously

10) _____ obstinate

A. an institution for the care of the mentally ill or those requiring special assistance

B. stubborn; unyielding

C. angry

D. sarcastically; humorously

E. unable to speak

F. perplexed; confused

G. having a worn or exhausted appearance

H. unhappy; lonely; sad

I. unending

J. neglected; messy

Fill in the blanks using words from the box below.

flashbacks	stage directions	dramatic irony	protagonist
antagonist	climax	internal conflict	external conflict
dialogue	theme		

11) Annie's struggle to let go of her past and stop feeling guilty about her brother's death is an example of _____.

12) James acts as a(n) _____ by trying to discourage Annie from teaching Helen.

13) The audience understands Helen's character and actions through the playwright's use of _____.

14) _____ occurs when the audience knows something that one or more characters in a play do not.

15) The audience understands Annie's difficult childhood through _____ in which Annie hears voices of people from her past.

16) One _____ of the play is that the value of an individual should never be underestimated.

17) The _____ of the play occurs at the end, when Helen finally realizes what language is and that words have meaning.

Choose the correct answers.

18) _____ What is Captain Keller's initial reaction to Annie?
   A. He believes that she will be able to teach Helen.
   B. He expresses prejudice against her because of her age, her disability, and where she is from.
   C. He thinks that Annie is a pushover and will not be able to control Helen.
   D. He feels threatened by her.

19) _____ How does James Keller feel about Helen throughout most of the play?
   A. He thinks that she is unable to learn anything, that she can only imitate motions.
   B. He feels that she has the potential to learn.
   C. He enjoys spending time with her.
   D. He feels sorry for her.

20) _____ How do Helen's parents treat her?
   A. They discipline her when she behaves badly.
   B. They are too harsh with her and expect too much from her.
   C. They try to teach her the difference between right and wrong.
   D. They give her everything she wants to keep her from throwing tantrums.

21) _____ Why does Annie bring Helen to the garden house for two weeks?
   A. Annie wants Helen to be completely dependent on her so that Helen will learn to communicate.
   B. Annie wants to discipline Helen for misbehaving.
   C. Annie wants to keep Helen from harming any of the other children.
   D. Annie thinks that Helen is sick and needs to be isolated from others.

22) _____ Which of the following is true about the asylum where Annie grew up?
   A. It was filled with rats and diseased women and men.
   B. It was the place where she learned how to read.
   C. She formed many friendships with the women there.
   D. She has returned to the asylum on many occasions.

23) _____ Which character shows a change by defending Annie in front of Captain Keller at the end of the play?

    A. Viney   B. Aunt Ev   C. James Keller   D. Mr. Anagnos

24) _____ Which of the following characters overcomes an internal conflict, learns to let go of the past, and is a changed person at the end of the play?

    A. Kate   B. Annie   C. Captain Keller   D. Viney

25) _____ What do Annie's last spoken words indicate?

    A. She has given up on teaching Helen.

    B. She regrets that she was not able to teach Helen more.

    C. She has finally learned to love another person.

    D. She does not want to continue teaching Helen.

Check   **Correct**   **Recheck**

You must now prepare for the Unit Test.
- Review the Objectives and Vocabulary for each Lesson.
- Reread each Lesson and its corresponding questions.
- Review and study the Quizzes and Unit Practice Test.

When you are ready, turn in your Unit and request your Unit Test.